My
GOD

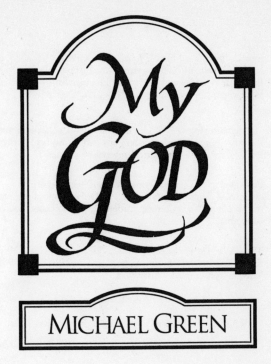

My God

MICHAEL GREEN

OLIVER
NELSON

THOMAS NELSON PUBLISHERS
Nashville

Published in Nashville, Tennessee, by Oliver-Nelson Books, a
division of Thomas Nelson, Inc., Publishers, and distributed
in Canada by Word Communications, Ltd., Richmond, British
Columbia.

The Bible version used in this publication is THE NEW
KING JAMES VERSION. Copyright © 1979, 1980, 1982,
Thomas Nelson, Inc., Publishers.

Printed in the United States of America.

Library of Congress Cataloging-in-Publication Data

Green, Michael, 1930–
    My God / Michael Green.
        p.   cm.
    ISBN 0-8407-9266-2
    1. God—Proof.   2. God—Love.   I. Title.
BT102.G743   1993
231—dc20   93-8568
                                                            CIP

1 2 3 4 5 6 — 98 97 96 95 94 93

Contents

The Forbidden Subject

*T*oday, in the West, we mention God only in times of crisis. "My God!" we exclaim when amazed, frustrated, or angry; "God help us!" we cry when the plane is about to crash. But those times apart, God hardly figures in our thoughts or conversations. He has replaced sex as the unmentionable subject. Indeed, both God and sex have been dragged down to the gutter in the vocabulary of casual swearing. But just go to a social gathering and try to start a serious conversation about Him—and see what reaction you get! Embarrassment, laughter, even hostility.

Yes, God is the forbidden subject these days. But this is a very temporary and local turn of events. Throughout history, belief in God has dominated human thought and culture, art, medicine, and science. And still today the vast majority of people in the world believe firmly in God. Atheists are a statistically microscopic proportion of humankind. Islam brings God into every aspect of life, public and private. Hindu temples are apparent everywhere in the East and have an enormous influence on the people. Christianity is dynamic and dominant in much of Africa, Asia, and Latin America. Religion is one of the most powerful forces in twentieth-century life—as it always has been.

"So what?" you may be saying. "I don't believe in God, and that's the end of the matter." But your believing a thing to be true or false does not, of course, make it so. Belief that a right-of-way exists across private land is of no benefit if you are wrong and the landowner decides to prosecute you. Millions believed that the earth was flat, yet it was a globe all the time. We await scientific verification or disproof of the Loch Ness monster; whatever the findings, either supporters or skeptics will find their beliefs shattered.

If God does not exist, belief will not produce Him; if He does exist, disbelief will not banish Him from the scene. So your disbelief in God is not necessarily the end of the matter at all. Belief should be based on evidence, right? But many people base their beliefs not on evidence but on custom, prejudice, wishful thinking, or superstition. Surveys show that more Americans, for example, believe in UFOs than in evolution. But this does not tell us anything important about either UFOs or evolution. It would only do so if we knew something about the quality of the evidence involved.

This book is an invitation to think seriously about God, to examine the evidence for and against believing in Him, and to evaluate some common arguments and theories about Him. That might seem a rather dry, academic prospect. But one factor lifts the whole discussion out of the realm of the academic and makes it deeply personal to every human being on the planet, and it is this: God is personal. He is alive. He cares about each one of us. It is possible to establish a relationship with Him. And He expects a response. Indeed, He holds us accountable for the response we make.

"How can you make such a claim?" you may well ask. Well, there is powerful evidence for my assertion. It is anchored in history—indeed, in the person after whom history itself is dated: Jesus Christ. The historical Jesus provides the strongest possible proof that God exists, cares, and comes to seek us out.

There is good contemporary evidence for the Roman occupation of Britain in 55 B.C. under Julius Caesar. It happened. I add it to the catalogue of other historical events of which my mind is full, and apart from occasional moments when the information is useful, it makes no difference to the way I think or live my life. But the evidence for the life, death, and resurrection of Jesus (which is, incidentally, much better documented than that for Caesar's invasion of Britain) cannot be treated in the same way. If I believe it, I cannot just file it away. It changed the world, and it cannot but change me.

So may I ask you to lay aside the prejudices

that so easily prevent us from facing up to this most important of all issues?

It may well be that nobody in your family or circle believes in God. But you are an adult: think for yourself! It may well be that you have been hurt by religious people or institutions. That is very sad, but it is an inadequate reason for refusing to consider the existence and claims of God. I may have been hurt by some Democrats or some Republicans, but that does not absolve me from looking into their politics and voting! A creed must not be judged simply by the failings of its adherents.

Perhaps you have a horrible suspicion that if you took God seriously, it would affect your life-style. It probably would! But take heart. If God is real and loving, He is not out to rob you and make your life miserable.

It could be that like many others, you have never looked deeply into the question of God. Life is too full of more pressing concerns— yes? Well, it is unwise to neglect the big issues of life, like where we came from, what life is worth, and where we are headed. Why not strike while the iron is hot, and look into it now?

Let's begin by facing up thoughtfully to some of the problems in the way of faith—and then move on more briefly to some of the practical questions to which it gives rise.

PART 1

Problems
and
Objections

1
I'm Not the Religious Type

The Religious Type

"No, Pastor, you'll have to find someone else to talk to. I'm afraid I'm not the religious type." How often you hear people say things like that! I have a lot of sympathy for them. There is something creepy and sanctimonious about that phrase "the religious type." I think of businesspeople in black suits, sitting in church pews at the funeral of one of their colleagues, trying to imitate "the religious type" for half an hour—then emerging breathless from the funeral into the open air in order to light a cigarette and return to normality.

For many people, religion is summed up by two very different images. One is presented regularly by the church choir, resplendent in its robes, immaculate in its singing, but somehow sounding very bogus. The other image is to be found in a great stadium, where the evangelist is urging people to come to the front for counseling; that can seem to be a mere playing on the religious emotions. The response of those who look on is often a rather relieved "I'm not the religious type."

Hypocrisy

Why do we so strongly dislike the religious type? Is it because we have almost come to regard religion and hypocrisy as the same thing?

It's a problem with a very long history. In Isaiah's day, back in the eighth century B.C., men and women were offering God all manner of sacrifices, but their hearts were far from Him. In Jesus' day, the scribes and Pharisees gained a reputation for being hypocrites. Many of them must have been absolutely genuine. Some, however, took care to be seen making long prayers in order to impress others, to give ostentatiously so that everyone would think how generous they were, and to make a great show of their biblical knowledge in order to shame others. Piety outside and corruption inside are a revolting mixture. Jesus had to accuse some of His hearers of being just like that: He said they reminded Him of the white sepulchers that were such a common sight on the hills, set against the deep blue of the Sea of Galilee. They looked marvelous from the outside, but inside they were full of corruption and dead men's bones.

The link between religion and hypocrisy did not die in the first century. Think of the hypocrisy in those very pious days of the Victorian era: the immorality that flourished, the exploitation that went on alongside meticulous religious observance. And rightly or wrongly, many suspect that the churchgoing figures among the whites in South Africa conceal hypocrisy, and that there is a good deal of it among the conspicuously church-oriented middle class in America. Could this be a sort of insurance policy to preserve the regimes against the inroads of black power and communism? I do not know. But I do know that many people assert very forcefully that they are not the religious type because they hate hypocrisy; yet they feel that somehow it is an essential part of religion.

Begging

Closely allied to this is begging. None of us likes being confronted by a beggar. It makes us feel uncomfortable; indeed, we feel "got at." We avert our eyes from the people who sit on the streets in our large cities with signs asking for money. But organized religion bears the image of the beggar. How many churches do you pass with a notice outside inviting you to save this historic building? How many churches do you go into with a notice inside telling you how much per minute it costs to run the place, and suggesting a minimum donation per visitor—a thinly disguised entrance fee?

I take the force of all this. That is why I admitted at the outset that I have a lot of sympathy for people who say they are not the religious type. But all the same I think they are wrong.

Clearing the Air

First, let me clear the air and have a look at those very reasonable objections to the religious type that have just been raised. It is true that a lot of bad things have been done in the name of religion. So they have in the name of medicine, too, but that does not mean we never go near a doctor. A lot of good things have been done in the name of religion, too, but that by itself does not make it true.

There is only one proper question for people of integrity: Is the religious account of the world and humanity true? If it is, then I want it, however many bad things have sheltered under its umbrella. I want to throw the bad things out into the rain but not to take down the umbrella.

It is perfectly true that some expressions of religion border on the nauseating—though we must always remind ourselves that what is nauseating to one person is meat and drink to another. I personally get switched off very fast by televised services. Others get annoyed by prayer meetings, evangelistic rallies, or Episcopalian matins. I have no doubt that there is a great deal of insincerity in church circles, and I have no doubt that illicit psychological pressure is exerted by some evangelists.

But once again, back to the basic facts. Did they, or did they not, happen? Was Jesus, or was He not, the Son of God? Did He, or did He not, rise from the dead? If He did, then I can afford to be broad-minded about types of religious expression I personally dislike. If not, then the whole lot is garbage, a type of escapism for which I have no time at all.

As for hypocrisy and money grabbing, these need not detain us long. Just because there are counterfeit coins in circulation, that does not stop you from using money, does it? Were there no "good" money, nobody would bother with counterfeiting it. So the existence of hypocrisy in religious circles is no reason for rejecting religion. It suggests rather strongly that there is a genuine article as well as all the spurious copies. Take a good hard look at Jesus in the Gospels. There is not a sniff of hypocrisy about Him. He was the first to denounce it in others. And it is with Jesus that we are concerned. Following Him means following the One who denounced hypocrisy and would have no part in it at all. Just because some of His followers have failed to live up to that standard, it does not stop you from making a better stab at it.

As for money grabbing, I believe that the church has all too often deserved its appalling image. It does give the impression that it is out for money—often through thoughtless insensitivity, such as when an offering plate is placed before visitors who may only visit the church once and, for all their hosts know, may well be financially committed elsewhere.

The proclamation of the Christian church, far from being a statement of financial needs, ought to be that it has found great treasures in Jesus Christ, and that unlike most treasures this one is for free. Jesus was always impressing upon people that entry into the kingdom of God or the Great Supper or friendship with

Him (all three add up to the same thing) was absolutely free—for black and white, Jew and Gentile, prostitute and Pharisee alike. Free: there is no entrance fee or service charge. Don't let the church prevent you from discovering the most wonderful person in the world, Jesus Himself.

Having, I hope, cleared the air, I now want to ask some pertinent questions of any who are hiding behind this "I'm not the religious type" motto.

Is There a Religious Type?

First let me ask you, Can you honestly say there is a religious type? Don't pretend it is comprised of the effeminate, the retired, and the addleheaded. I think of some of the people in the Oxford church I used to serve: a leading gynecologist, a factory worker, a librarian, a horticulturist, a garage owner, a builder, an architect, an engineer, a man who had been finding God in prison, a lawyer, an atomic scientist, a university teacher, several unemployed people, hundreds of students (the majority of whom are studying scientific subjects), members from Iran and India, Sri Lanka and South Africa (black and white), the U.S.A., Canada and Sweden, Germany and Hong Kong, Japan and Australia, Kenya and Uganda, Sudan and Nigeria. The diversity of their attitudes, their temperaments, their ages, their interests, their everything, is so vast that it would be ridiculous to class them all as the religious type. These Christians are not just one type; they are all types— extrovert and introvert, tough and weak, old and young, black and white. Their diversity has only one unifying factor, but that factor is strong as steel: Jesus Christ.

Can you say that the first disciples of Jesus were the religious type? Perhaps a mystic like John could be described like that, but what of rugged fishermen like Andrew and Peter? What of freedom fighters like Judas Iscariot and Simon the Zealot? What of money-grabbing tax collectors like Matthew? What of the drunkards at Corinth who became

Christians? What of the thieves and magicians at Ephesus? It is ludicrous to suppose that the people who first followed Jesus belonged to the religious type. The Jews, in fact, had a very fine word for the religious type and another, far from complimentary, for the ordinary folk, "the people of the land." All Jesus' first followers came from this latter group: all were the nonreligious type.

A Nonreligious Faith

Don't let your dislike of religion keep you away from Jesus. In a very real sense He came to destroy religion. The German martyr Dietrich Bonhoeffer was not playing with words when he coined the phrase "religionless Christianity." That is precisely what Christianity is. It is not an attempt by good-living people to please God and win a place in heaven. It is God coming in His love and generosity to seek folk who would never seek Him, holding out His arms to them on a cross, and saying, "Come to Me, and let us share life together." Not a religion, but a rescue.

That is why the earliest Christians were so keen to stress that they had no temple, no altars, no priests. They had no religion, in the normally accepted sense of that term; hence, the Romans called them atheists. Instead, they had a Person, who knew them, loved them, and never left them. Nothing could separate them from His loving presence. So prayer became not a ritual but conversation with a Friend. Worship was not a ceremony for Sundays but the natural outpouring of love and adoration to the Savior by His people when they met together. They needed no church buildings, for where two or three were gathered together in His name, He was in their midst as He had promised He would be. They needed no priests, for Jesus had opened immediate, equal access to God's presence for every one of them.

Christianity, properly understood, is the most earthy of faiths: it does not separate the secular from the sacred but keeps the two firmly together. The Lord is as interested in what I do at eleven o'clock on Monday in my daily work as He is in what I do at eleven o'clock on Sunday in a church service.

Yes, Christianity is for nonreligious people. It is not going too far to say that if you insist on being religious, you will find Christianity hard; in fact, you will find it almost impossible.

You will find it almost impossible to *become* a Christian, in the first place, because your "religion" will get in the way; you will feel that somehow you are better and more pleasing to God than your irreligious neighbor, which is just what the Pharisees felt—and that is what kept them away from Jesus.

And you will find it almost impossible to *be* a Christian because once again your "religion" will get in the way; you will feel that the Christian life depends on your religious observances, not on the Lord. You will be inclined to keep a little religious corner in your life for God and not allow Him to have the whole thing. Yes, you will find it much harder to become—and to be—a Christian than the person who is not the religious type.

The matter of truth

And now a few other questions for the man or woman who is not religious.

Are you concerned about the truth? That is a vital question. Do I hear you say, "Of course I am"? Very well, then, you and the Christian are interested in exactly the same thing. Jesus claimed, "I am . . . the truth" (John 14:6). He claimed, in other words, to be ultimate reality in personal, human terms. If you are interested in what is ultimate and what is real, then you cannot remain disinterested in Jesus. You may examine His claims and dismiss them as untrue; what you cannot do, if you maintain a deep concern for truth, is to pay Him no attention, to shrug your shoulders and say, "I'm not the religious type."

The matter of courage

Next question: Have you the courage of your convictions? I once met an atheist at a discussion group, an able man doing doctoral studies in physics. When we were talking together at the end of the meeting, I asked him if he had ever read one of the Gospels with an open mind, willing to respond to Christ if and when he was convinced by what he read. His reply surprised me, but on reflection I think it may be true of many others. He said, "I dare not." What a remarkable admission! The man was used to assessing material, making judgments, committing himself to theories in physics on the ground of the evidence; yet he was afraid to do the same with the New Testament material in case it should convince him and draw him to the Christ he was evading. Surely, if he had the courage of his atheistic convictions, he should have been quite willing to read the Gospels. It would have given him firsthand material to make fun of when arguing with his believing friends. But no. He did not have the courage of his convictions.

In point of fact, atheists are statistically a tiny minority. The vast majority of people across the world and throughout the ages have found belief in God the best explanation of themselves and of their world. There are good reasons for this almost universal belief in

God. Some of them are presented in this book. They are not theories. They are facts. And they are worth weighing, both individually and cumulatively.

The matter of cost

The next question is very similar: Dare you take your stand with Jesus? He warned potential disciples to sit down and count the cost of what following Him would mean. Were they prepared to stand with ten thousand men against an opposition force of twenty thousand? If not, they would have to make humiliating peace terms in double-quick time. It is not pleasant to admit that you are wrong about the basic issues of life and death. Not easy to join the despised Christian company. Not easy to put up with being mocked at work for your allegiance to Christ. Not easy to allow Christ to affect your morality. Of course it is not!

Jesus never said it would be easy. He said that following Him meant death as well as life. Death to the old way of living, then accepting new life, new power, new standards from the Lord. All this is very tough. Many people dress up their cowardice in other terms, such as indifference—"I'm not the religious type." But cowardice it remains. The man of Nazareth is too demanding, too uncompromising, too loving, too upright for the soft and compromising, the lazy and those who like to go with the crowd.

The matter of fulfillment

Another question I would like to ask the person who is not interested in religion: Do you want to find fulfillment? Jesus once described the kingdom of God as finding treasure. Imagine a farmer plowing his field, drearily, monotonously, without any special expectations. Then his plow hits a box. He investigates and finds to his amazement that the box is full of diamonds and rubies. Whose heart would not beat faster at such a discovery? That, Jesus implied, is what discovering God's kingdom is like. For the kingdom is brought to us in the person of the King, and the King is Jesus. Really, then, it is nothing to do with religion and its demands and observances.

The Christian life is concerned with relationships. First comes the restoration of our relationship with God, then the restoration of our links with others, as the basic harmony brought by Christ spreads outward. Relationships are among the most precious things in life. Yet, all too often they are spoiled by selfishness, racial prejudice, jealousy, or pride. Jesus Christ unites people and brings harmony where once there was discord, and that spells fulfillment at the deepest level of all.

I think of a painfully shy student who found a living faith in Christ during his first weekend at the university. Within six weeks he had opened up like a flower and was relating with far greater freedom to others. I think of a couple whose marriage was on the point of breaking up when both partners were brought to faith in Jesus. The new relationship with Christ brought them closer together than ever before, and their marriage is now strong and happy. I think of a soldier, loathed for his bigheadedness and rudeness, whose whole attitude to others changed radically when he allowed Jesus Christ to take control of him. I think of two schoolboys, who could not stand each other until both of them found Christ during the same summer holidays; thereafter, relationships were on a completely new plane (I should know, for I was one of the boys).

This same Jesus draws together those whom every pressure in the world is driving apart. He does it in Northern Ireland as genuine believers (as opposed to the religious type, be they Protestant or Catholic) meet across the border at night and pray for each other, support each other's widows, and tend each other's wounded. He does it in the Middle East as He brings together in one fellowship of true believers those political irreconcilables, Jews and Arabs. He does it in South Africa, between white and black believers. I have seen it time and again with my own eyes. But I know no other force on earth that can do the same. Jesus is treasure indeed, for He brings fulfillment to all our relationships, once we allow Him to repair our relationship with God.

The matter of destiny

There is one other question I would like to ask the man or woman who is not interested in religion: Are you interested in your future?

Who is not? Our education, our aspirations, our qualification seeking, and our hunger for promotion are all geared to this end—securing a better future. A significant sector of the advertising industry is devoted to selling us a prosperous future. Financial management and investment companies paint a glowing picture of leisured, prosperous retirement or a time even earlier when, if we invest in the advertiser's product or service, we will have everything we ever wanted and all the time in the world to enjoy it. But what happens when we get it? Is there not an emptiness at the top? Money does not satisfy permanently, nor does sex, nor does fame, nor does manipulating others. And many of the people at the top know it. The actress Raquel Welch put it well:

> I had acquired everything I wanted, yet I was totally miserable. . . . I thought it was very peculiar that I had acquired everything I had wanted as a child—wealth, fame and accomplishment in my career. I had beautiful children, and a life style that seemed terrific, yet I was totally and miserably unhappy. I found it very frightening that one could acquire all these things and still be so miserable.

After all, what is life about? Are we bound for extinction, or is there some life beyond the grave? If you are really concerned for your future, you can scarcely avoid considering the matter of final destiny. Pascal put it at its most entertaining when he suggested that the afterlife is like a wager. If you believe in God, you are at no disadvantage in this life and at considerable advantage in the next. If you do not believe, but find in the next that there was a next, you are most unfortunate!

But to be more serious. What sense is there in shutting your eyes to the one Person who is well attested as having broken the grip of death and having come back to tell us not only that there is an afterlife but how to get there? In business or commerce it would be accounted sheer folly to go for short-term gains and neglect capital appreciation—or depreciation. Yet that is just what people do who take no thought for life after death. They go for short-term goals and prefer not to notice the fact that their capital, their life, is depreciating toward zero when it could if rightly invested appreciate indefinitely. By the way, the vocabulary of financial management is not inappropriate; the New Testament borrows a number of words from business Greek.

Christians assert, not just on the basis of documents written two thousand years ago, but on the basis of continuing worldwide experience, that Jesus of Nazareth has broken the ultimate barrier in our universe: death. They may be right; they may not. You must decide that after investigation. But to shrug off the whole matter saying, "I'm not the religious type," is sheer folly if you think at all seriously about your future.

Faith Has Two Sides

Sometimes people say, "I'm not the religious type," with a touch of wistfulness, as if what they were really saying was, "I wish I had your faith." My answer to that is simple. You can have my faith. Faith is nothing other than trust; and trust, to be any good, must have two sides to it. First, there needs to be good evidence of trustworthiness; then there needs to be genuine commitment. It is as simple as that. You have faith in a Boeing airplane when you fly, do you not? That means that in your opinion Boeing is eminently reliable; it also means that you are prepared to entrust yourself to the company's trustworthiness. So it is with Christianity. You need first to be convinced that there is a God, that He cares about us, that He has revealed Himself in Jesus Christ, and that it is possible for you to get in touch with Him.

Then you need to entrust yourself to His trustworthiness.

In the following pages we will consider some aspects of what faith in Jesus Christ involves. I hope that as we consider them together you will be helped to appreciate the trustworthiness of God and also encouraged to entrust yourself to it. Then you *will* have my faith. Then you will be able to say, "I'm not the religious type, but I think I have discovered the key to the universe."

2
Belief in God Is Intellectual Suicide!

God Is Out of Fashion

Despite the opinion polls, which show that the vast majority of people in Western countries (not to mention almost everyone in the East) do believe in God, it is amazing how often you hear the question of the Almighty dismissed in a single sentence: "Oh, you can't believe in God these days." It seems intellectual suicide.

Very understandable, in a way. We live in a very busy age, and many of us have neither the time nor the inclination to inquire into abstruse subjects that do not directly concern us. When Dr. Watson first met Sherlock Holmes, he was astonished to find that Holmes knew nothing about the solar system and had no idea that the earth traveled around the sun. Holmes retorted that the information was irrelevant to him: "If we went round the moon it would not make a pennyworth of difference to me or to my work." Many of us would say the same: great issues of science may be irrelevant to our daily lives and may safely be left to those whose business it is to know about such things.

But what if there is a God who made us, loves us, and will judge us? Well, if that is the case, then—as Dr. Jowett, famous head of an Oxford college, once put it—"It is not what I think of God, but what God thinks of me that matters."

However, the idea of God has been so abused in the past that we tend to shy away from it. God has been portrayed as the man in the sky with the big stick. We have been told to be good and to do the right thing because God will judge us if we offend Him. "God's will" has been found to be a very useful tool for keeping people in their places:

> The rich man in his castle,
> The poor man at his gate;

God made them high and lowly,
And ordered their estate.

A whole system of social and racial oppression has been founded on that view of God, quoted here as it is expressed in one of the verses (which is now usually omitted!) of the hymn "All Things Bright and Beautiful." God's will is something that certain people in certain ages have claimed to be so sure about that they have engaged in religious wars (like the Crusades) or religious persecutions (like the Inquisition) to press their point. God has, furthermore, been used as a sort of plug to fill gaps in scientific knowledge. Even Newton postulated God to keep the universe and its laws going. But as scientific knowledge has grown, the gaps have shrunk, and God with them. Napoleon once read a fashionable work on the nature of the universe and expressed to its author, Pierre-Simon Laplace, his surprise at finding in it no mention of God. "Sir," Laplace thundered proudly, "I had no need of that hypothesis."

For all these reasons, God is out of fashion. As *Time* magazine headlined on its cover some years back: "God Is Dead!" But it is difficult to be sure about these things. Perhaps there is as much fashion as there is reason about it all. Just four years later, the headlines of *Time* were asking: "Is God Coming to Life Again?"

After all, you get no justification for religious wars or inquisitions in the Bible. You do not find this handbook of Christianity maintaining that you should do good in case God should punish you for your failures. God is nowhere used in the Bible to plug the gaps in human knowledge; rather, He is portrayed as the source and sustainer and goal of the whole universe, including human beings and our knowledge.

Perhaps we ought to look a little more closely at the claim that you can't believe these days. What is so special about these days that makes it harder for us to believe in God than it was for our ancestors? Here are four of the most common problems.

The problem of science

First, there's the astonishing success of science. In the past fifty years, the whole face of the world has changed. When my father was a boy, there were no cars, no airplanes, and most people never moved more than a few miles from their own village. The change to space exploration, nuclear technology, and the global village has all happened in his lifetime. No wonder people are confused. Science would seem to have won the day. No wonder many people pin all their hopes on it and discard the idea of God. Sir Richard Gregory wrote his own epitaph:

My grandfather preached the gospel of Christ.
My father preached the gospel of socialism.
I preach the gospel of science.

In point of fact, there is no battle between an informed belief in God and the assured results of science. The fathers of modern science, men like Kepler, Galileo, Copernicus, and Bacon, were earnest believers in God. They saw God's revelation in Scripture and in the natural world as complementary. Kepler, for instance, asserted, "The tongue of God and the finger of God cannot clash." The Cavendish Laboratory in Cambridge has inscribed above its entrance: "The works of the Lord are great, sought out by all who have pleasure therein." And contrary to the belief of many, there is a high proportion of believing Christians among the leading scientists of the world.

Belief in a Creator sets out to explain the great Mind behind all matter. There is no necessary contradiction between that belief and scientific theory. Interestingly enough, the biblical account of God's creation tells us something of the One who created and something of why He did it. But it does not set out to tell us how. What it does say clearly, however, is that behind the creature lies the Creator, and that we are not only "of the dust of the ground" (i.e., part of the physical universe) but are also in some sense infused with "the breath of life" and made in the Creator's image.

No discoveries in the realm of how life developed can repudiate that claim. If someone were to discover how to create life in a laboratory, that would not put God out of business. It would simply show that when brilliant minds take matter (with real living matter to copy, incidentally) and arrange it in a very special way, a living particle may come into existence. In other words, matter arranged by intelligent minds can produce life. Exactly what Christians have always claimed for God! If we discover the secret of life, we shall merely be thinking the Creator's thoughts after Him.

Nothing in the scientific method can either demonstrate God's existence or disprove it. But for what it is worth, the basic presupposition of the scientific method strongly supports the existence of a Mind behind matter. It is axiomatic for all scientific inquiry that there are order and purpose in the physical world. Why should this be if the world sprang from chance and chaos? There are very few pure materialists around these days, for it is abundantly obvious that analysis of physical laws and chemical constituents cannot explain human behavior, reason, emotion, wonder, speech, morals, and worship. "There are more things in heaven and earth than are dreamed of in your philosophy"—these words of Shakespeare are applicable to the person who tries to make scientific materialism the only arbiter of truth. There is nothing in scientific procedure that need embarrass any believer in God the Creator.

The problem of suffering

Second, there's the problem of suffering. Not that it is greater than ever before, but it seems greater. Every night TV brings images of suffering into our living rooms. In many parts of the world brutal wars are in progress, with terrible consequences for human lives and social structures, and the details of the suffering are brought to our eyes meticulously and unsparingly, sometimes in live broadcasts that present us with a front-row seat at the precise time the tragedy is taking place. Perhaps we in the television era are tempted to ask much more trenchantly than did our predecessors: How can there be a God if He allows all this pain and anguish in His world?

I do not want to minimize this problem for one moment. It is by far the strongest argument against the existence of God. But suppose, for a minute, that the problem of pain drives you to reject God's existence and to imagine that some monster rules our destinies or that the stars are in charge of our fortunes. How does that help? You may have gotten rid of the problem of evil and pain (though you still have to live with them), but you have replaced them with a much bigger problem. Where do kindness and humanity, love and unselfishness, gentleness and goodness come from in a world that is governed by a horrid monster or uncaring stars? No, there is no help from that direction.

As a matter of fact, the Christian has greater insight into the insoluble problem of suffering (and it remains insoluble, whatever philosophy of life you take up) than anyone else has. The Scriptures teach us that God is no stranger to pain. He did not start the world off and leave it callously to its own devices. He does not willingly afflict us and take delight in torturing us. The very reverse. He cares so much about the agony and pain of this struggling world of His that He has gotten involved in it personally. He came as a man among men. He lived in squalor and suffering; He knew thirst and hunger, flogging and heartbreak, fear and despair. His life ended in one of the most excruciating ways known to humanity. Let nobody tell me God doesn't care! Let nobody claim that the boss doesn't know what life is like on the shop floor!

The image of the incarnate, suffering Christ has fascinated both religious and secular people for centuries. People are drawn to the wonder of it, the gratuitous generosity of God, even when they only dimly understand it.

Take a long, hard look at the cross. Through that cross, God is saying to you that He does care about pain. He cares passionately and selflessly. He cares so much that He came to share it. He is forever the suffering God. The cross tells me that God loves me even in the midst of pain and suffering; when on the cross everything looked its blackest, Jesus was still the supreme object of His heavenly Father's love.

Moreover, through that cross, I can vaguely discern another truth: that God uses pain. He turns evil into good. For it was evil, real evil, that crucified Jesus; and yet, by the way He took it, He overcame evil. He turned hatred to love in some, at least, of His persecutors. He gave an example of innocent, uncomplaining suffering, which has inspired humankind ever since and enabled men like Bishop Wilson to win the hearts of some of the men who tortured him in a Japanese prison camp in the Second World War, by means of his courage and spirit.

And what makes such overcoming of pain possible? Not merely the cross of Jesus as an example to follow. You need more than an example in the midst of agony. Something else about the cross has rubbed off on Christians ever since. It is the sense of victory. On the first Good Friday, Jesus died with a cry of triumph on His lips: triumph over pain and hatred, suffering and death. And that was not the end. He rose from the chill grip of the tomb on the third day. From that moment onward, He has enjoyed the power of an endless life.

Christians are people who have put their trust in Him, come to know Him, and begun to taste the power of His risen and endless life. How is it that the early Christians could look cheerfully at death in the arena as they faced wild beasts and gladiators? How could they face being roasted on a grid? Simply because they were convinced that evil and pain had suffered ultimate defeat through what God did on that cross of Calvary and in the resulting resurrection. Even death was a defeated foe. So they came to look on suffering not as an unmitigated evil but as an evil that had been conquered by their suffering and triumphant God; an evil that He could even use to discipline them, to refine them, and to equip them for further usefulness and deeper Christlikeness.

And the suffering but victorious God, the sinless but sin-bearing God, has given on the cross of Christ a trailer of His future film. They could safely leave Him to give fuller light on it all in the life to come, knowing that it would be a further explanation of the mystery of the cross where, in the very midst of history, God showed that He cared about pain, shared it, and overcame it. That is why the Christian need not be worried that suffering in the world makes belief in God impossible. It is only belief in a suffering God that stops us from either becoming totally callous or going out of our minds at all the suffering that afflicts our world.

The problem of meaninglessness

Third, there's the problem of meaninglessness. Never before in human history has there been such a widespread belief that in the end nothing matters; we came from nothing, and we go to nothing. No values are implanted in us because there is no God to implant them. No part of the human frame survives death because there is no eternity. Meaning has disappeared from life. More money, more leisure, yes. But don't talk to us about meaning in life because there isn't any. A leading modern painter, Francis Bacon, writes,

> Man now realises that he is an accident, that he is a completely futile being, that he has to play out the game without reason. Earlier artists were still conditioned by certain types of religious possibilities, which man now, you could say, has had cancelled out for him. Man can now only attempt to beguile himself for a time by prolonging his life—by buying a kind of immortality through the doctors. . . . The artist must really deepen the game to be any good at all, so that he can make life a bit more exciting.

What, in fact, the artist has done is to bring home this meaninglessness to every level of society. It comes through films and pop music. It is everywhere. Dirk Bogarde said, as his career took off, "I rather liked it all. There was one wavering doubt, however, just one. Who...was I? There was a vast vacuum, and in spite of a house, car, all my family and possessions, I belonged nowhere." As Pink Floyd put it in their famous song, you're "just another brick in the wall." If Pink Floyd is not your scene, turn to a Nobel Prize winner and hear Jacques Monod proclaim, "The universe was not pregnant with life, nor the biosphere with meaning. Our number came up in the Monte Carlo game." It reminds me of words on a French gravestone: "Here lies a man who went out of the world without knowing why he came into it."

It's a theme, too, that runs through much modern comedy. The Monty Python team were philosophically very close to the theater of the absurd, with its zany elaboration of the basic thesis that life has no purpose or meaning; the bizarre absurdity of their comedy is an expression of a view of what reality actually is. In his brilliant stage play *Rosencrantz and Guildenstern Are Dead*, Tom Stoppard has a character reflect upon life before his arbitrary extinction: "But why? Was it for all this? Who are we that so much should converge on our little deaths? . . . To be told so little—to such an end—and still, finally, to be denied an explanation."

Now if you are eaten up with this philosophy of meaninglessness, of course you won't find any sense in God talk. But it is a chicken and egg situation. The philosophy of meaninglessness is an attempt by modern existentialists to cope with the full consequences of atheism. Deny God, and then see if you can make sense of everything else. The truth is that you can't.

But try it the other way around. What if there is a God? Then the world is not a mere fluke; it is the result of His creation. Humanity is not junk but God's deputy on this earth. History is not bunk but God's story struggling for expression through all the follies of humankind. Life is to be understood not simply in terms of the threescore years and ten but as a training ground for being with God forever. No longer need we be torn between the very obvious order and purpose in nature and the purposelessness, meaninglessness, and lostness that we modern humans find in our hearts. If only we will return to the Creator of order and purpose in nature, we will begin to find order coming through into our own lives and a sense of purpose in cooperating with the Creator in the management of His world.

The problem of proof

The fourth problem is the matter of proof. "You can't prove God," they say, as if anybody could. That's perfectly true. You can't. You can't prove that your mother loves you, either. In fact, you can prove precious few things, and they are by no means the most interesting things in life. To prove a thing really means to show that it could not be otherwise, which is a very final form of certainty. You cannot prove that you are alive. You cannot prove the link between cause and effect that runs through every action we do. You cannot prove that you are the same person you were ten years ago. The brilliant philosopher David

Hume attempted to prove the link between cause and effect and between himself as he then was and himself ten years previously, and he failed. Failed utterly.

Proof is applicable only to very rarefied areas of philosophy and mathematics, and even here there is debate. For the most part, we are driven to acting on good evidence without the luxury of proof. There is good evidence for the link between cause and effect. There is good evidence that the sun will rise tomorrow. There is good reason to believe that I am the same man as I was ten years ago. There is good reason to suppose that my mother really loves me and is not just fattening me up for the moment when she will pop arsenic into my coffee. And there is good reason to believe in God. Very good reason. Not conclusive proof—but very good reason, just the same. Let me introduce you to the evidence. Let me outline to you why I believe it is much harder to reject the existence of a Supreme Being than to accept it. Here are six facts, which all point the same way. They point to God.

1. The fact of the world

Look at the fact of the world in which we live. So far as we know at present, this planet is the only part of the universe where there is life. But what accounts for this world of ours? Whatever view of cosmic origins we opt for, we are driven to ask not merely *how* but *why*. The natural world itself—the "book of nature," as earlier Christians sometimes called it—argues powerfully for God's existence by posing very demanding questions: What accounts for our world? Why is there something rather than nothing? Can our world be the result of some cosmic accident?

It simply will not do to put the whole thing down to chance. The existence of the cosmos is not just one of those things. If the world came about by chance, how is it that cause and effect are built into that world at every turn? Huxley, the great scientist, once said, "The link between cause and effect is the chief article in the scientist's creed." It is not very rational to believe that chance gives birth to cause and effect! And it is no more rational to argue that a world based on cause and effect was itself random and uncaused.

A noted biologist once observed that the likelihood of the world being produced by chance is about as great as that of an explosion in a printing shop producing the complete works of Shakespeare! He was right.

If the world is not an accident, then it must have come from somewhere. Science itself, the record of the systematic observation of the world, drives us—if we really think about it—to belief in a Creator, a source outside itself. We call that source God.

2. The fact of design in the world

Look at the fact of design. At every level the world of nature shows evidence of the most intricate design. Think of the birds' migratory ability, the caterpillar's metamorphosis, the focusing equipment of an eye, the structure of freezing that allows fish to breathe under the ice, the radar of a bat, the built-in gyroscope of a swallow, the camouflage of a nesting pheasant. They all show careful design. And where you have design, you have a Designer. Or think of the perfect harmony of the laws of physics. Reflect on the marvel of conception and birth. At every point there is evidence of a great Designer.

When you look at the Bayeux tapestry, you do not jump to the conclusion that it just gradually evolved without any intelligent supervision. You know that someone supervised its development. But the Bayeux tapestry is child's play compared with the infinite variety displayed in the tapestry of nature.

If conditions on earth had been the slightest bit different, life would have been impossible. Our environment shows signs of meticulous design. In hot countries, bees have a way of coping with hornets that have the unpleasant habit of haunting their hives and biting off their heads. The bees emerge in a rush from the hive, surround the hornets, and move their wings so fast that a great heat is worked up. When it reaches 46°C, the hornets die. If the temperature were to go up to 48°C, the bees would die, too. But it does not. This speaks of design, not chance.

Even John Stuart Mill, a strong opponent of Christianity, came to the conclusion at the end of his life that "the argument from design is irresistible. Nature does testify to its Creator." Einstein, too, spoke of his "humble admiration for the illimitably superior Spirit who reveals himself in the slight details which we can perceive with our frail mind." After Einstein had propounded his theory of relativity, and after its general acceptance following the Michelson-Morley experiment, the experiment was repeated and gave different results. But nobody doubted the relativity theory! Everyone assumed (rightly as it turned out) that the results must be due to experimental error because the theory was too good, *too rational,* to be false. In other words, the physicists themselves were operating on the assumption of design in the universe, however much they might have claimed to be following merely experimental results.

Very well, then, if there is design in the world, where did it come from? Not from us. We don't lay down the laws of nature or design the development of the fetus in the womb. It looks very much as though a Designer is at work.

Long ago William Paley developed the argument by using the illustration of a watch. It runs something like this:

> See this watch? Well, in the old days people used to believe that a watchmaker had made it. The cogs, the pinions, the glass and numbers all bore the marks of intelligent design. But now we have grown out of that sort of thing. We know that a watch has gradually evolved. There is no design about it! Natural selection has slowly eliminated all elements that are irrelevant to watches. The metal has coalesced, the glass has grown over, the cogs have gradually developed, and last of all the strap grew.

Put like this, it is not difficult to see how ridiculous the argument is; the man who advanced it would be ignored, if not consigned to a mental hospital! Yet precisely the same argument is advanced about the world itself by sane men and women who think they are being both reasonable and avant-garde. To attribute marks of design to blind evolution makes no more sense in the case of the world than it does in the case of the watch. Paley's argument has been attacked on the ground that God is not a watchmaker. True, but Paley never said He was. God is far more than a watchmaker if He is God at all. But He is assuredly not less!

The argument from design is extremely persuasive, and to say with Jean-Paul Sartre, "This world is not the product of intelligence. It meets our gaze as would a crumpled piece of paper. . . . What is man but a little puddle of water whose freedom is death?" is to shut your eyes to one of the clearest indications that there is a Creator God who has not left Himself without witness.

The psalmist was right three thousand years ago when he sang, "The heavens declare the glory of God; and the firmament shows His handiwork" (Ps. 19:1). And so is another assertion to be found in the Psalms: "The fool has said in his heart, 'There is no God'" (14:1).

3. The fact of personality

The most complex of all God's creations is humankind itself, described in the Bible as the image of God, yet apparently infinitely varied and inexhaustibly fascinating—capable of the glories of a Mozart or a Shakespeare, able to affect the environment for good or ill; the master of the microscope, the designer of the spacecraft.

Human beings have the power to reason. We are able to make up our minds about what is true and false. We are also creative, able to arrange objects and ideas in new ways. We can have insights. Some philosophers argue that reason and creativity are nothing but physically-based brain processes, conditioned reflexes responding to stimuli. But if that were true, how could we know it? That argument itself along with our ability to understand it would be a product of those same conditioned reflexes. It would have no cogency whatever.

It is much more rational to believe that reason and creativity are gifts of the supremely creative Intelligence we call God.

Our physical bodies comprise a nonmaterial thing, the mind, which enables us to make sense of the physical world. It points us to God, who is also nonmaterial and who is at work in our physical world.

Look at the fact of personality. It is one of the most remarkable phenomena in the world. We cannot precisely define personality, but we know well enough what we mean by it. The difference between a person and a thing, between a live person and a dead one, is fundamental. Personality is the vital quality that makes us different from a corpse, a robot, an animal, or a chemical.

When Sartre, in the quotation given above, denied that the world was created by Intelligence, he was insulting not only his Maker but his own power of reasoning. He was saying, in effect, that there was no reason to believe what he was saying! The fact is that we are not mere automatons; there is more to us than that—human personality. Some thinkers are so reluctant to believe this that they have advanced the improbable creed of materialism, seeking to reduce everything in life to what can be measured scientifically. In other words, other people are merely developed blobs of protoplasm. So am I. I have no future, no authentic existence. I think I am a conscious, rational being who can mix with others like me. But no. Science, as such, knows nothing of rationality and consciousness, of personality and sociability. It deals with molecules and magnetism, elements and electricity, things that can be counted and measured. The "I" has no place in such language. If that is the ultimate language of reality, then I cannot describe myself, and I am driven to the conclusion that I, as a sentient, intelligent being, do not exist.

Not very plausible. But the alternative is disturbing. It suggests that my personality cannot be explained simply in terms of its physical components. I am more than matter. Very well, but how come, if there is no God? Can the personal come from the impersonal? Can human beings emerge from brute matter? Does a river run higher than its source? Of course not. Then how do we get human personality out of the inorganic matter that is the elementary stuff of which our universe is entirely composed, according to the materialist? Can rationality and life spring from chance and nonbeing?

No, the fact of human personality is another impressive pointer to the God who created us in His image. All attempts to derive our intelligence, joys, and loves from mere matter are totally unconvincing. To claim that we are just a collection of atoms, a bunch of grown-up genes, is not only to fly in the face of the evidence; it is the ultimate trashing of human dignity. This is not to say that God is restricted to a personality like ours, but it is to say that the ultimate source of our being is not less than personal.

Only one explanation of human personality makes sense—and that is, that we come from a personal source. That source of human personality we call God. In fact, human personality is one of the strongest evidences of His existence. And that is precisely what the Bible teaches: "God created man in His own image . . . male and female He created them" (Gen. 1:27).

4. The fact of values

Look at the fact of values. Nearly all the world's major religions have a broad agreement in the area of values. They are against stealing, immorality, greed, hatred, murder, and lying. They are for responsibility, truth, honesty, faithfulness, and helping others. How are we to explain this common mind?

We all have values, but they are very hard to understand if there is no God. After all, you don't expect to find values knocking around in molecules! Matter does not give rise to morals. So modern godless people are confused about where our values fit in. We value life—but why should we if life really springs from chance, from a random combination of atoms? We value truth—but why should we if there is no ultimate reality? We value goodness—but what is that doing in a world derived from plankton? Indeed, what do we mean by goodness if we are all conditioned to behave in a certain way anyhow? We revel in beauty—but there is nothing in it since it, too, springs from the chaos in which our world originated. We value communication—but the universe is silent.

Yes, we have our values. But they do not accord very well with the atheist's picture of the world. With God left entirely out of the reckoning, they must spring instead from chance, matter, and millions of years to allow for extensive developments. I do not find much basis for value judgments there.

But what if there is a Creator God? Then our values make sense. They are planted within us by God, the supreme Value, and each of them sheds light on some aspect of His nature. So life is valuable because it is His greatest gift; hence, the infinite value of every individual. Truth matters because it is one aspect of God, the ultimate reality. Beauty and goodness are likewise two of the faces of God, and every good action or beautiful sight is an inkling of the good and beautiful source from which they come. Best of all, we do not inhabit a silent planet. God has spoken and revealed Himself, to some extent at least, in the world, in its design, in values, and in human personality. When we communicate,

it is not vain jabbering but a God-given ability entrusted to us by the great Communicator
Himself.

Those are two basic attitudes to values. I
know which makes more sense to me. John
Lucas, the Oxford philosopher, develops this
argument clearly and simply:

I want to do well. But it is impossible to do
well unless there are values independent of
me by which my performance can be assessed.
I cannot want to do only what I want to do,
or I am denying my nature as a rational agent.
The existence of values is a pointer to God
which it is hard, indeed, to evade.

5. The fact of conscience

Look at the fact of conscience. Conscience
is universal. We all know that there is a difference between right and wrong, however much
we may try to deny it to justify doing what we
want. Conscience is a pointer to God if ever
there was one! Your conscience doesn't argue.
It acts like a lawgiver inside you, acquitting

you or condemning you. It doesn't say, "Do this because you will gain by it," or "Do it because you will escape trouble that way." It just says, "Do it." It is a most remarkable pointer to the God who put it there.

Conscience is not an infallible guide, but it points to standards that we ought to keep. The word *ought* derives from *owe to*. To whom do we owe this obedience? The inner law strongly suggests a Lawgiver. We struggle to refute so uncomfortable a notion. But no other explanation of conscience has ever been found convincing.

Oh, of course, conscience is not the voice of God, straight and simple. It has been warped by all sorts of things: our environment, our rationalizations, our disobedience. But equally certainly, conscience cannot be some form of self-interest; that would not account for noble acts of self-sacrifice. Nor can conscience be explained away as the pressure of society, as mere social conditioning. Often it drives people to go against the attitudes of their peers "for conscience' sake." It was not from any pressure by society that John Newton and William Wilberforce conscientiously fought for the liberation of slaves or Martin Luther King, Jr., championed the cause of Afro-Americans. Their actions were carried out in the teeth of opposition by society, and so it has always been with every moral advance.

Despite the diversity of human cultures the world over, there is, as we have seen, a remarkable agreement on the essential values to which conscience points: the general condemnation of murder and theft, of adultery and lust, of hijacking and hate. There is universal agreement that peace is right and war is wrong; that love is right and hate is wrong— however little we manage to carry it out in practice. And it is conscience that points us to this difference between right and wrong, and the claim that right has upon us. C. S. Lewis summed it up like this: "If no set of moral ideas were better than another, there would be no sense in preferring civilised morality to Nazi morality. The moment you say one lot of morals is better than another, you are in fact measuring them by an ultimate standard."

Even the great thinker Bertrand Russell, who during his earlier career fought tooth and nail against the idea of an ultimate distinction between right and wrong, said, toward the end of his life, "To love is right, to hate is wrong." But how does he get such moral absolutes in what he claimed is a godless world? It doesn't add up. You do not locate principles of conscience in a chance collection of atoms, which is all the world consists of if you remove the possibility of a Creator.

Atheists have a great deal of trouble in explaining that moral imperative we call conscience. The obvious answer is that it is a powerful pointer to a holy God who put it there in our hearts because He is deeply concerned for our behavior. Morality, conscience, the difference between right and wrong—all are important indicators of a God who is interested in what is right and good and true.

And God is no blind force, no abstruse

designer. He is personal, and He is so concerned with what is right that He has equipped every one of His human creatures with a moral direction finder: the conscience. It is a very plain indicator both of His existence and of His moral concern.

6. The fact of religion

Look at the fact of religion. We are religious animals. Everywhere in the world, all through history, men and women have worshiped God. Their perception of God has been varied, but worship has been constant. The very earliest human beings left behind them remnants of temples and altars. In the sixth century B.C., philosophers in Greece poured scorn on religion and invited people to grow up. Religion continued. And so it has done everywhere in the world ever since.

The Russians sought to abolish religion after the Revolution in 1917. They failed. They tried again with violent persecution under Stalin. They failed. Despite strenuous efforts to eliminate religion in Communist countries during the past seventy years and to replace it with the worship of Lenin or Mao, the Christian faith is flourishing in those countries. It has proved one of the major factors in glasnost, which has changed the face of Eastern Europe. And now the gospel has free course in Russia!

People are incurably religious. They are going to worship God or a pseudogod, but worship something they will, whether it is something abstract, like the idea of progress, or physical, like material prosperity. Materialists, of course, are very much worshipers—they direct all their work and attention and assign supreme value to things that are very transient. It is a form of worship, of "giving worth."

One fact about human beings has distinguished us since our first appearance on earth. It marks us as different from all other creatures. That is, we are creatures who worship. Wherever we have existed, there are the remains, in some form or other, of worship. That's not a pious conclusion; it's an observed fact. And all through history when we've deprived ourselves of that, we've gone to pieces. Many people nowadays are going to pieces, or they find the first convenient prop to tie their instincts on to. It's behind the extraordinary adulation of royalty. It's behind the mobbing of TV stars. If you don't give expression to an instinct, you've got to sublimate it or go out of your mind.

Such is the conclusion not of a philosopher or a priest but of a novelist, Winston Graham in *The Sleeping Partner*. He's right, isn't he? Worship is a deeply rooted instinct. Nobody can stop religion because human beings were made to worship. We must worship either God or idols; and it matters not whether those idols are of wood and stone, as in primitive cultures, or of ambition, wealth, and sex, as in more sophisticated societies.

What are we to say, then? Is worship the only one of our instincts that has no reality to satisfy it? Food satisfies our hunger drive; intercourse, our sexual drive; sleep, our drive for rest. Isn't it reasonable to suppose that our drive to worship was put in our hearts by God Himself, the only possible reality that can completely satisfy it?

These are some of the facts that not only make belief in God reasonable but make it very hard to rationally deny His existence. Each makes more sense if God exists than if He does not. Together they point compellingly to a God who is skillful, skillful enough to design the courses of the stars and the development of a fetus. They point to a God who is the source of human personality and, therefore, not less than personal, however much He may transcend all that we mean by that word. He is the ultimate source of our values: life, language, truth, beauty, and goodness find their ultimate home in Him. He is so concerned about right and wrong that He has furnished each of His creatures with a conscience. And He wants us to know Him and to enjoy Him, to worship and to live in His company—hence, the universal religious instinct of men and women through history and all over the world.

But He still remains the unknown God. How are we to discover any more about Him?

Perhaps those who say that all religions lead to God are right. It's a possibility worth considering. Let us do so in our next chapter.

3
All Religions
Lead to God

An Attractive Theory

Until a few years ago, comparative religion was a study for the handful of experts who busied themselves in such an odd subject. Now it is replacing the study of theology in universities all over the Western world and has a firm niche in religious instruction in schools. The reason, of course, is that we have at last awakened to the fact that the world is a global village, and the presence of Asians, Indians, Japanese, and Vietnamese in the U.S. has meant that the question of other religions has been brought much closer.

For practical reasons, certainly, comparative religion enables us to understand more fully the cultural and religious heritage of our neighbors. But there is an element of curiosity, too. What are we to make of these other faiths? Presumably, they are all much of a muchness. Presumably, they are all pathways to God, and you might as well take your pick among the smorgasbord of religions.

Such a view has immense attractions. It avoids a black-and-white choice and sees everything as shades of gray. It is essentially tolerant, and tolerance is a very fashionable virtue. It is modest and does not make strong pretensions for your own chosen religion. Democratically, we take the views of everybody and try to build up an Identikit picture of God. It seems admirable common sense. And some extremely significant people and organizations back it up. For example, the saintly Indian leader Mahatma Gandhi once said, "The soul of religions is one, but it is encased in a multitude of forms. . . . Truth is the exclusive property of no single scripture. . . . I cannot ascribe exclusive divinity to Jesus. He is as divine as Krishna or Rama or Mohammed or Zoroaster."

But this view won't do for two compelling reasons.

It's illogical

It is a lovely sentimental idea to suppose that all religions are basically one, and that they all represent variations on a common theme. It summons up a picture of the human race as one big, happy family, all honoring the same universal Father in a multitude of national and cultural ways. But unfortunately, such a vision flies in the face of all the evidence. How can all religions lead to God when they are so different? The god of Hinduism is plural and impersonal. The god of Islam is singular and personal. The God of Christianity is the Creator of the world. The divine in Buddhism is not personal and is not creative. You could scarcely have a greater contrast than that.

Christianity teaches that God both forgives us and gives us supernatural aid. In Buddhism there are no forgiveness and no supernatural aid. The goal of all existence in Buddhism is nirvana, extinction—attained by the Buddha after no less than 547 lives. The goal of all existence in Christianity is to know God and enjoy Him forever. The use of images figures prominently in Hinduism; Judaism prohibits making any image of God. Islam allows a man four wives; Christianity, one.

Perhaps the greatest difference of all lies between the teachings of the Bible—which assert that none of us can save ourselves and make ourselves pleasing to God—and those of almost all the other faiths, which assert that by keeping their teachings a person can achieve fulfillment or be saved or reborn or made whole. Nothing spells out this contrast more powerfully than the Buddhist story, which starts off so like the parable of the prodigal son. The boy comes home and is met by the father, and then has to work off the penalty for his past misdeeds by years of servitude to his father. The principle of karma (cause and effect, paying off your guilt) is poles apart from grace (free forgiveness when you don't deserve it at all).

I do not at this point want to evaluate different religious faiths. I just want to show how utterly illogical it is to say that they all point in the same direction. It is as foolish to say that all roads from Denver lead to New York. They do nothing of the sort, and it is not helpful in the least to pretend that they do. They lead to radically different destinations. Heaven or extinction; pardon or paying it off; a personal God or an impersonal monad; salvation by grace or by works—the contrasts are irreconcilable.

The trouble is that today's tolerance has reached the point where it is no longer a virtue but a vice. It is a cruel casualness toward truth. It is no kindness to anyone if we tell all people that their views are as true as anyone else's. We simply display our cynicism, as if we said to a blind person sitting on the edge of a precipice, "It doesn't matter which way you move. All paths lead to the same goal."

People no longer set out their beliefs in a marketplace but put them on shelves in a museum. When the centrality of truth is set aside, differences between religions are no longer urgent contradictions whose resolution is vital but mere curiosities of cultural diversity.

Bishop Lesslie Newbigin maintains that the great divide among religions is in their attitude toward history. Most religions are like a wheel:

> The cycle of birth, growth, decay and death through which plants, animals, human beings and institutions all pass suggests a rotating wheel—ever in movement yet ever returning upon itself. . . . [So] dispute among the different "ways" is pointless; all that matters is that those who follow them should find their way to that timeless, motionless centre where all is peace, and where one can understand all the endless movement which makes up human history—understand that it goes nowhere and means nothing.

The other great symbol is not a wheel but a road. This is the view of Judaism and Christianity. Newbigin expresses it thus:

History is a journey, a pilgrimage. We do not yet see the goal, but we believe in it and seek it. The movement in which we are involved is not meaningless movement; it is movement towards a goal. The goal . . . is not a timeless reality hidden behind the multiplicity and change which we experience. It is yet to be achieved; it lies at the end of the road.

That is the uniqueness of the Christian claim. God has intervened in history. The history of the Jewish people and the birth of Jesus, His cross, and His resurrection are milestones along the road that does not return to its starting point but ends in heaven.

Not only, however, is it illogical to suppose that all religions lead to God; it is impossible.

It's impossible

There are two reasons why it is impossible for us to find God through whatever religion you care to name. The first is the nature of God.

If there is a God, then He is the source

both of ourselves and of our environment. He is the Lord over all human life:

> Have you not known?
> Have you not heard?
> Has it not been told you from the beginning? . . .
> It is He who sits above the circle of the earth,
> And its inhabitants are like grasshoppers. . . .
> With whom did He take counsel, and who
>   instructed Him,
> And taught Him in the path of justice?
> Who taught Him knowledge,
> And showed Him the way of understanding?
> Behold, the nations are as a drop in a bucket,
> And are counted as the small dust on the
>   scales;
> Look, He lifts up the isles as a very little
>   thing (Isa. 40:21-22, 14-15).

That is the God we are talking about. How can we possibly climb up to Him? How can the cup understand the potter who made it? It cannot be done. Mere mortals cannot find God, however hard we search. Religion, all religion, is bound to fail.

To be sure, we can have a go at it. But how far does it get us? The facts we considered in the last chapter are some help but, frankly, not much. The fact of the world indicates an outside cause. Design in the world suggests this cause's intelligence. The fact of human life suggests that this cause is not only intelligent but personal. Conscience indicates His concern about right conduct, and values such as truth, beauty, and goodness may have their origin in Him. The fact that no nation in the world has lived without belief in God suggests that God wants our worship.

But so what? He remains the unknown God. You can get so far by inference but no further. After that you need to hear from Him or meet Him—or both. The creature cannot possibly discover the Creator unless He chooses to disclose Himself. That is one reason why all religions are bound to disappoint. And as a matter of fact, that is precisely what they all do.

Christopher Mayhew published a book some years ago entitled *Men in Search of God.* In it, representatives of various world religions gave their account of their religious experience and their search for God. Not surprisingly, none of them claimed to have found Him. It was the same when Ronald Eyre presented a television documentary series about religion entitled "The Long Search." "How futile!" commented Dick Lucas:

> The long search indeed! When I open the Bible I don't find the sheep is having a long search to reach the shepherd. Imagine it finding its way back at the right time and place. Who's doing the searching in the New Testament? Not man, not the philosopher, the twentieth-century enquirer, the television programme, nine grand programmes ending in cliche and waffle. It's the Shepherd looking for the sheep. Yes: there is a long search. And the one who instituted it is God.

If by "religion" we mean our search for the divine, it is bound to fail. What we need is not to compare the chinks of light that each of us may have grasped but to have the day dawn. We need not a religion but a revelation. And that is precisely what Christianity claims to be: a revelation from God. Unlike other holy books, the Bible does not pretend that we are seeking God; it tells us about the God who comes in search of us.

No through road

There is a second reason why religion will never win through to God. Not simply because of the nature of God but because of the nature of human beings. The Bible gives a pretty unflattering picture of men and women, but one that is uncomfortably near the mark. It tells us several unpleasant truths.

For instance, it informs us that we are not the earnest lovers of God that we would like to suppose ourselves to be; on the contrary, we are enemies in our minds "by wicked works" (Col. 1:21). We do not have the hearts of gold that we like to think we have; on the contrary, "the heart is deceitful above all things, and desperately wicked" (Jer. 17:9). It tells us that we are not impartial in our search for the truth; on the contrary, people "suppress the truth in unrighteousness" (Rom. 1:18). We do not follow every gleam of light that comes our way; on the contrary, people love "darkness rather than light, because their deeds [are] evil" (John 3:19).

There seems to be a basic twist in human nature that makes us allergic to welcoming the best when we see it. More often than not, we want to get rid of it because it shows us up. One of the more pathetic illusions of humanism is that we are all good guys at heart, and given decent environment, decent working conditions, plenty of money, and secure employment, we will all be good citizens, and the heart of gold will shine out. What nonsense! If we are all good guys at heart, why does the crime rate go up every year, along with our prosperity?

Take London, for example. There crime has increased twentyfold in the last fifty years, and one survey revealed that 90 percent of London's youngsters under sixteen admitted they had at some time or other engaged in theft. And is New York any better?

If we were all good folk at heart, we would flock to the best person there has ever been, Jesus Christ. But anyone who has had any experience in evangelism, in bringing others to share in the joy of the Christian life, knows what a battle generally ensues before the person in question finally gives in to Christ. I have seen "good" people sweating with the intensity of their struggle to keep clear of the Light of the World. Francis Thompson knew what he was talking about in that poem of his, "The Hound of Heaven," which begins,

I fled Him, down the nights and down the days;
  I fled Him, down the arches of the years;
I fled Him, down the labyrinthine ways
  Of my own mind; and in the mist of tears
I hid from Him, and under running laughter.

The very fact that we hide from Him shows that we are self-centered creatures at heart, just as the Bible says we are. And we have another closely allied problem. Something is wrong with our will. We don't seem to be able to live up even to our own occasional efforts after high standards. How long do your New Year's resolutions last, for instance? How long do the peace and goodwill of the Christmas period continue in your office? Or how many times have you given up overeating? Jesus put His finger on the trouble when He said, "Whoever commits sin is a slave of sin" (John 8:34). It's true.

No wonder Paul comes to the conclusion that the Old Testament had reached before him, as he draws to the end of his shattering indictment of contemporary pagan and religious society:

There is none righteous, no, not one;
There is none who understands;
There is none who seeks after God (Rom. 3:10–11).

The myth is exploded. We are not honest seekers after God. Most of us, most of the time, are only too thankful to keep out of His way. All of us are disqualified, whether we come from the so-called Christian West, the former Communist bloc, or the mystic East. None has arrived at God because He is too great for any of His creatures to reach Him and because His creatures are too twisted, too self-centered, to want to. The greatness of God and human sinfulness are two massive barriers to our supposing that all religions lead to God. All religions do not lead to God. None of them do.

Only One Hope

There is only one hope, and that is the possibility of revelation. We cannot reach God, but there is no reason why He should not reach us. That consideration escaped the celebrated Herbert Spencer, a leading nineteenth-century agnostic. He maintained, sensibly enough, that no one has ever been known to penetrate with his finite mind the veil that hides the mind of the Infinite. He concluded, accordingly, that the Infinite could not be known by the finite, and that agnosticism was therefore secure. Not at all!

There is no reason why the Infinite should not make Himself known to the finite, and the Bible gives the account of the only faith claiming He has done precisely that.

A revelation

Suppose for a moment you were God. The people you made have turned their backs on you. They do not want to share their lives with you. They want to go their own way. What are you to do? You might start with a likely individual and work on him and his descendants. God did that: the likely individual was called Abraham. He trusted God, obeyed Him, and became the father of the Jewish nation. But that nation strayed from the path Abraham had trodden. What was to be done? Perhaps a time of hardship in a foreign and oppressive country might make them come to their senses? That is what Israel's time in Egypt was all about, and later on the medicine had to be repeated in the Babylonian exile. You might raise up prophets to call the people back to you. God did just that, too. "Listen to the words of My servants the prophets," says the Lord, "whom I sent to you, rising early and sending them, but you have not listened" (see Jer. 25:4). Finally, if you cared enough, you might come in person, for a visit, after your staff had sufficiently prepared the way. That, too, God did—at the first Christmas.

The way was as prepared as it could be. The Jewish nation, after two thousand years of history, was passionately persuaded that there was one God and no runners-up. The Roman Empire had secured peace throughout the known world. The Greek language was universal, and its culture pervasive. The stage was set for the maximum impact of God's personal visit. And so the One called Jesus ("God to the rescue"), or Immanuel ("God is with us"), was born. The God who, over many centuries and in many different ways, had spoken through His prophets to the people had at last spoken a clear, final, and decisive message, not through a prophet but in the person of His Son. At long last men and women could see that God is, God speaks, God cares. No longer is He the unknown

God. "No one has seen God at any time. The only begotten Son, who is in the bosom of the Father, He has declared Him," was how one eyewitness summed up the matter (John 1:18). Jesus shows us in terms of a human life what God is like. That was the first purpose of His coming to our world, to bring us the revelation of God without which we would still be fumbling vainly in the dark.

A rescue

His coming had a second purpose as well, closely linked with the first. For when human beings saw that perfect life of uprightness and love, the highest and the best imaginable, they nailed Him to a cross. He was too uncomfortable a person to be allowed to go on living. His was too blazing a light. The natural instinct of humankind—who likes living in the dark—was, and is, to extinguish that embarrassing light. The people did not succeed, of course—"the light shines in the darkness, and the darkness did not comprehend it" (John 1:5)—but they had a very good try.

Do you see what happened? The coming of Jesus did not merely show us what God is like. It also showed us what we are like. John wrote, "Men loved darkness rather than light, because their deeds were evil" (John 3:19). And if you want commentary on that verse, ask yourself what would happen to the circulation of the Sunday papers if they started recording acts of virtue rather than deeds of vice! There you have clear evidence that we love darkness rather than light.

So we human beings need something more basic even than a revelation from God. We need a rescue by God. Our understanding *and* our will are at fault. Jesus came to rectify both. He showed us what God was like by His incomparable life. He put us right with God by His sacrificial death. That is why the cross is the symbol of Christianity. It is the most important achievement in the whole of His life, indeed, in the whole of history.

There Jesus, the God-man, took responsibility for human sin in its totality. Christ "suffered once for sins, the just for the unjust, that He might bring us to God," says one eyewitness (1 Pet. 3:18). "In this is love, not that we loved God, but that He loved us and sent His Son to be the propitiation for our sins," writes another (1 John 4:10). Another New Testament writer cries out in exultation: "There is therefore now no condemnation to those who are in Christ Jesus" (Rom. 8:1) because "God did by sending His own Son in the likeness of sinful flesh, on account of sin: He condemned sin in the flesh [i.e., of Christ]" (Rom. 8:3).

Wherever you look in the New Testament, you find the same truth, however variously it is expressed. In the pictorial language of the book of Revelation, you find it put like this:

[I saw] a great multitude which no one could number, of all nations, tribes, peoples, and tongues, standing before the throne and before the Lamb, clothed with white robes, with palm branches in their hands, and crying out with a loud voice, saying, "Salvation belongs to our God who sits on the throne, and to the Lamb!" (7:9–10).

Nothing like it

The symbolism is plain. These people, from every background in the world, are praising God in heaven and thanking Him for His rescue operation that covers the scruffy clothes of their fancied goodness with the perfect white robe of Christ's righteousness. As the writer goes on to say a few verses later: "These are the ones who... washed their robes and made them white in the blood [i.e., the death] of the Lamb [i.e., Jesus, willingly sacrificed for them]." A rescue operation indeed. Where else in the religions of the world do you hear of a God who undertakes salvation for His people by personally bearing responsibility for their wickedness and allowing it to crush Him?

But even that is not all. The God who has revealed Himself and rescued us has done it for a purpose. Amazingly, He wants to relate to us. That is where the Resurrection comes in. He is no dead figure in a history book, two thousand years out of date. He is alive, and we can have dealings with Him.

I remember vividly the day when this truth became a reality to me. I asked the Risen One to come and live in me. He has done so. I have not found God. I could not if I wanted to, and I would not have wanted to anyway, so self-centered was I. But He has found me. He came to earth to reveal Himself to me. He died to remove the beastliness of my wrongdoing. He lives and is at work changing my life from the inside. And all this I find to be very good news. No other faith does anything remotely like this. No other faith claims to. Christianity is quite distinct from other religions. It is a case not of human beings in search of God but of God in search of human beings. Not a religion at all but a revelation and a rescue.

It is at this point that an important question arises.

"If you are right about Jesus, are other religions all wrong?"

By no means. The God who made the world, the God who revealed Himself in Christ, has not left Himself without witness in the world. Every good thought, every gleam of light, every word of truth to be found in any religion, and in atheistic philosophies like Marxism as well, is part of God's self-disclosure. All truth is God's truth and has its focus in the One who became incarnate. So Christians welcome truth wherever it is found.

As you look into other faiths, you will find an enormous amount that is true and worthy, that is moral and good, as well as much that is not. But you will not find anything good and true that cannot be found in Christ. You will not hear from them about a God who cares for you enough to die for you, to rise from the grave as a pledge of your future, and to be willing to come and share your life with you. You will not find in any other faith a revelation of God in fully personal terms, a rescue of humankind from self-centeredness and sin, and the offer by this God to come and indwell the life of every man, woman, or child who welcomes Him.

It is not that Christians are narrow-minded about other faiths. But if Jesus is, as the Resurrection indicates, God Himself come to our rescue, then it is crass folly to reject Him. And this is something that we can investigate for ourselves. We are not dealing with myth and legend, of the sort that makes it impossible to know when Buddha lived (estimates vary between 1000 and 500 B.C.) or details of his birth. We are dealing with history. There is plenty of documentary evidence to establish the claim that Jesus of Nazareth rose from the dead on the first Easter in A.D. 30 or 31 and launched the Christian community.

His scattered followers did not expect it. To begin with, they did not believe it. But they were driven to do so by their experience of the risen Jesus, and once they were convinced, nothing could silence them. They had discovered the key to life. They did not claim merely that a corpse had been resuscitated. That would not have done much good. They believed that almighty God shared our nature as the man Jesus, that He suffered and died, and that even death could not hold Him! His resurrection says yes to His claim to be "the way, the truth, and the life" (John 14:6). His resurrection vindicates His claim to deity.

In the risen Jesus, God confronts us with shattering directness. He offers us total aid; but He demands of us total obedience. It is splendid to have an interest in comparative religion. But the more you know of other faiths, the more you see Christianity to be unique. And the key to Christianity is the Resurrection.

I have investigated the reliability of the Resurrection with some care in two books, *The Day Death Died* and *The Empty Cross of Jesus*, where extensive evidence for the historical event is set out. Here we need to make only one point, and it is this: Christianity is a historical religion. It claims that God has taken the risk of involving Himself in human history, and the evidence is there for us to examine with the utmost rigor. The facts will stand any amount of critical examination. No book on earth has been subjected to such prolonged and detailed scrutiny by some of the best minds in the world over many hundreds of years as the New Testament has been. Examine the evidence for yourself, and do not rely on secondhand opinions either from those who believe the Christian story or from those who reject it.

This is the most important issue you will ever have to decide. Did Jesus rise from the dead or not? If not, then there will be time enough to look to all the other faiths in the world, to see what help for living can be found in them. But if He did rise, and you are persuaded of it, then that settles for you the question of which religion. Christ can no longer appear to you as just a very fine man. Although fully human, He somehow brings God to you. And as God, He claims your loyal obedience.

PART 2

Questions

4
What Is
God Like?

We have just considered the sobering implications of the fact that all religions do not lead to God. But if so many concepts of God taught in the world's great religions are inadequate and, in part, dangerously misleading, what is the truth about God? Given that He exists, what is He like?

From our discussion in this book so far, we can say seven things about God, which are central to the Christian faith and for which there is very good evidence. Each one shows us something of what God must be like; taken together, they give us at least the beginnings of a portrait of God, even though it is bound to be incomplete.

God is mighty. He brought the whole cosmos into being. Before He made it, nothing existed at all.

God is wise. He has arranged with infinite skill every detail, small and great, of our incredibly complex universe.

God is rational and creative. As Einstein remarked, "God does not play dice with the universe," and He is not—as some ancient Greeks believed their gods to be—capricious and arbitrary. He is cosmic Mind, both constant and ceaselessly creative.

God is personal. He may well be beyond personality, but He is at least personal, for He is the source of our personality. Therefore, He understands us and can communicate with us.

God is good. In fact, He is the absolute source of goodness. All our highest and best values come from Him.

God cares about right and wrong. He hates evil and abominates wickedness, so much so that He has given us a conscience.

God wants our worship. He made us to know Him and enjoy Him forever. That is why He has put the religious instinct inside us, why He has "placed eternity in our minds." He knows that we cannot achieve our full potential and our highest good so long as we remain out of touch with Him. On the level of intellectual argument, that is an outline of what God is like.

But intellectual arguments are not enough. They may answer the hard questions our minds ask, but they do not really touch our deep personal needs, our fears and worries, our insecurities and loneliness, as we live in a world that at times seems to be falling apart.

If that is all we can know about God, then it is as if we were standing in the rain on a winter's day, believing that the sun is bright and warm up there somewhere but cut off from it by a heavy barrier of clouds. There is no way we can cut through the clouds by ourselves or break free from our prison into the sunshine. In the same way, if our experience of Christianity were merely cerebral, we would be left with nothing to deal with our emotional and spiritual needs; we would know in our minds that our hearts' needs were met but would be unable to turn the theory into practice.

We certainly wouldn't be able to achieve a deep, personal knowledge of God by ourselves. The only way would be if God took the initiative; if He revealed Himself to us; if He wrote to us; if, perhaps, He came to us.

Meet God!

Well, God has done just that!

The Bible is His message to humankind. It is our letter from God. And it provides striking confirmation of the things we have already inferred about God from the world and the people in it.

In the very first sentence of the Bible, God is revealed as the mighty Creator. Throughout its pages, He is shown to be the Sustainer who takes care of the universe and the infinitely wise One who keeps it all working harmoniously together; the laws of nature are His laws.

In the Bible, we are even given a picture of God holding out His hands day and night to the people He has made, longing for them to return from their selfish independence and make room for Him in their lives. He wants each one to have the fulfillment of knowing Him personally.

The Bible never tires of telling us about the goodness of God, His faithfulness to His children under all circumstances. In it, we read of a God who is looking for our worship and our loving obedience. Indeed, His top prescription for human happiness and fulfillment is to "love the Lord your God with all your heart, and your neighbor as yourself."

We see even more. In the Bible, we encounter a God who has infinite compassion for His creatures. He is passionately on the side of the poor, the outcast, those who are unjustly treated. He is full of steadfast love for us, even if we do not want to know Him or obey Him. That is what God is like. Of course, none of these facts about God can be absolutely proven. You cannot prove any of the really interesting things in life. They have to be experienced, not just reasoned about. But these Bible claims about what God is like are totally consistent with the picture that our world and our human nature give us about God. They all make sense.

5
What Has God Done for Me?

That's all very well, you may be thinking, *but whether in the Bible or in nature, God still seems so far away. What has He ever done for me?*

The Bible gives a wonderful answer to that question. Many religions think that God does not care very much, if at all, about human beings. In Buddhism, the divine is impersonal; it is unable to care. In Hinduism, the inexorable principle of karma operates; you get precisely what you deserve, and there is no compassion, no forgiveness. In Islam, Allah is compassionate but inscrutable; you cannot know whether or not he will have mercy. In many spirit-worshiping cultures, the gods take on the fearsome shape of terrifying animals and evil spirits, which must continually be appeased if disaster is to be kept at bay.

Only the Bible presents a God who loves and loves and loves. He loves so much that He did not only send us His message in Scripture; He came to us in person. That is the Christian claim. God came to find me when I did not particularly want to find Him. He did not come because I had done something to deserve it or because there was some excellence of character or unique ability that made me worthy of His coming. He loves me simply because He loves me. That is all He has told me. And He came in the only form I could really understand—a human life.

That is what Christians celebrate at Christmas. *Immanuel,* one of the names given to Jesus at His birth, means "God is with us." That name suggests who He is. The name by which He is most often known, *Jesus,* means literally "God to the rescue." That name shows us the reason for His coming. He came to rescue human beings from the consequences of our sins. Sins are nothing less than rebellion against God, the God who gave us life and who will call us to account one day.

That is the claim. God Himself has come to this world to rescue us from the mess we have gotten ourselves into. If it is true, then it is wonderful news, and none of us need be the least bit embarrassed to say with joy and gratitude, "My God!" If not, it is a shabby deceit. Real Christianity leaves no room for polite apathy. We should either embrace it whole-heartedly or attack it as a lie.

Jesus

The burden of proof is on Jesus. Is He, or is He not, "God to the rescue"? He was human all right. His birth and life and death are well chronicled. But was He more than human? Did He really bring God to us within the confines of a human life?

I believe He did. But I ought not to believe it without some very good evidence. That evidence is available for anyone to read and assess in the world's number one best-seller, the Bible. The whole of the New Testament is about this claim.

Here are some pieces of evidence derived from its pages. Think them over.

Jesus' impact on people

His appeal to young and old, rich and poor, educated and uneducated, rulers and subjects worldwide is without parallel. Many hundreds of millions all over the world today worship Him as God incarnate, and they have done so ever since He came—and changed B.C. (before Christ) to A.D. (*anno Domini:* the Year of the Lord).

Jesus' teaching

Soldiers were once sent to arrest Jesus. But they fell back in amazement and returned empty-handed, saying, "Nobody ever taught like this man." He taught, moreover, with His own authority, not quoting the philosophers and teachers who preceded Him, explaining, "My doctrine is not Mine, but His who sent

Me" (John 7:16). It is the most marvelous teaching the world has ever heard.

Jesus' miracles

They cannot be denied. They are attested in almost every strand of the New Testament and in Jewish writings as well. He healed the sick and even raised some people from the dead. He fed a crowd of five thousand from five little loaves of bread and two small fish. Yet the astonishing facts were never done for show; they were signs. The miracles were pointers to who He was.

Jesus' claims

Jesus claimed three things that ought to stop us in our tracks. He said that He could forgive sins. He accepted worship. And He told us that He would conduct the final judgment. All three characteristics belong unequivocally to God alone; only God has the right to do them. If Jesus' claims were true, it would mean that He really is "God with us."

If they were not, He would be a blasphemer, a deluded madman. But His actions showed that He was far from mad; He was the wisest, most balanced character who ever lived.

Jesus' death

Jesus claimed that His death was going to be a ransom for humanity. He meant that our self-centeredness had cut us off from God and had gotten us in its power. We could not bridge that gap or break that power. But in His incredible love, Jesus, who was utterly innocent and sinless, took on His own head the wickedness of the whole world. He made a way back to God for us by surrendering His own life in place of us, whose lives were forfeit. A "ransom" indeed.

Jesus' resurrection

On the first Easter, Jesus came back from the chill of the grave where He had been laid that previous Good Friday. He did not live on for a few years only to die again. No, that resurrection was eternal, unique, and undreamed of. Jesus not only carried the enormous load of human wickedness to the grave, but He broke the power of death and is alive forever.

Taken together, these pieces of evidence are very difficult to square with the notion that Jesus was just a great man. They point to One who really did bring God into our midst. God cared enough for us to come into our world and show us—through the life, death, and resurrection of Jesus—what He is really like. Never again will we be able to say, "What has God done for me?" He has done everything we could possibly need to rescue us from our selfish ways, bring us back to Him, and fill our lives with the power of His risen life.

6
What Difference Would Belief in God Make?

There is only one good reason for belief in God—because it is true. We do not believe in order to get some advantage or other. Nevertheless, when you can honestly say that God is your God, it makes a great deal of difference to your life.

God Gives Meaning to Our Lives

If we sprang from plankton and are heading for extinction, there can be no overall purpose or meaning in human life. That is why there is so much despair among modern artists, writers, and filmmakers. But if we are the product of a living God who plans to have a relationship with us throughout eternity, then this life is a time of training and preparation for a truly wonderful goal after we die. And while we are alive, there is tremendous fulfillment in seeking to please God in all we do.

God Gives Hope to Our Lives

Human beings cannot survive long without hope. And most of our hopes either disappoint or are very short-term. But if God exists, and you know Him, you can have utter confidence about the ultimate destiny of this world and of yourself. Once you know He has reached out to you, you can be sure He will never let you go. Apart from God, there is no long-term hope; every year you live past the age of twenty is over the hill and heads toward the unrelieved destiny of illness, death, and extinction.

God Gives Motivation to Our Lives

If there is no God, and I am on my own, there is nothing to restrain my innate selfishness. I can be nice to others if it pays me. If not, I can be a perfect brute, so long as I can get away with it. But not if God is alive and well, and I am in touch with Him! My delight will be to do His will and to reflect something of His generous, compassionate, wholesome character so dazzlingly displayed in Jesus Christ.

God Gives Enjoyment to Our Lives

It is a myth that the Christian life is dull. Far from it. It is the happiest life in the world. Jesus promised to give His joy and peace to His followers, and He does. So we can revel in our joys, knowing who is their ultimate source. We can appreciate beauty, truth, goodness, creativity, and the natural world all the more because we know that each displays something of His character or handiwork. Our pains and sorrows are lit up by the assurance that God would not allow anything to befall us that ruined His ultimate purposes of good for our lives. And when times are tough, we can cheerfully accept the discipline and purifying that shape our lives to be more like our Master, Jesus Christ.

God Gives Power to Our Lives

Once we are in touch with Him, we are not left to the best that our human resources are capable of. He offers to put a new moral strength into our lives so that we can begin to achieve the good things that had seemed so elusive and to live progressively more as we know we should. It is the very power that brought about Jesus' resurrection from the grave!

God Gives Profound Relationship

He does it in two ways. One is a marvelous sense of belonging to other believers wherever you go in the world. No society can match it. You may never have met the other Christians before, but the sense of being members of the same family, rescued by the same Lord, and indwelt by the same Spirit is unique and fantastic. The other way God does it is by giving us a relationship with Himself that no circumstance, no distance, no loneliness, can spoil. He promised that He would be with us always, right to the end of the world. And He is. True believers will testify to God's constant presence with them, which is an unspeakable comfort and strength.

God is Himself what Christians call Trinity. None of us fully understand it, but it is clearly taught in the Bible and reminds us that God is plurality within His unity. He is relationship. That is why our relationships are the most deeply satisfying things in life. You can't get more basic and more fulfilling than that. Ask two people in love if that is not true! Alas, the relationship of two people sometimes pales in the course of time, but the presence, the power, and the steadfast love of God never wane.

7

How Can It All Become Real?

Do you feel a growing frustration? You say, "I'm beginning to see that God is there and that He cares about me. I even believe that Jesus came to bring God to us and show us the way back to Him. But I still don't feel any closer to Him."

Well, it need not stay that way. Beginning a personal relationship with God is far from complicated.

Realize Your Value

Many people have very low opinions of themselves. But God does not share those views. We are so valuable in God's sight that He thought us worth coming to search out.

More, He thought us worth dying for. So each of us is of inestimable value to Him.

Give Up Your Rebellion

Our self-centeredness and rebellion against God distance us from Him. If we are to get back in touch, we must hand in our weapons and take His outstretched hand. This does not mean that we must try to make ourselves presentable before God will accept us. It does mean that we have to give up our normal, human attitude of rebellious independence and admit that our only hope is to be found in God's free pardon.

In his autobiography, *Surprised by Joy*, C. S. Lewis describes his conversion to Christianity:

> You must picture me alone in that room at Magdalen, night after night, feeling, whenever my mind lifted even for a second from my work, the steady, unrelenting approach of Him whom I so earnestly desired not to meet. That which I greatly feared had at last come

upon me. In the Trinity Term of 1929 I gave in, and admitted that God was God, and knelt and prayed: perhaps, that night, the most dejected and reluctant convert in all England. I did not see then what is now the most shining and obvious thing; the Divine humility which will accept a convert even on such terms. The Prodigal Son at least walked home on his own feet. But who can duly adore that Love which will open the high gates to a prodigal who is brought in kicking, struggling, resentful, and darting his eyes in every direction for a chance of escape?

Lewis illustrates very well the point made earlier: in the biblical picture, the Shepherd is seeking the sheep and not vice versa.

Understand God's Offer

As recorded in the New Testament book of Acts, the apostle Peter told an eager crowd, "Repent, and let every one of you be baptized in the name of Jesus Christ for the remission of sins; and you shall receive the gift of the

Holy Spirit" (2:38). If the listeners were willing to give up their rebellion, two wonderful gifts were on offer: forgiveness and the Holy Spirit.

Forgiveness was won for us on the cross when Jesus died and took responsibility for our guilt. It was terribly costly for Him, wonderfully free for us. Yet the hard part is putting aside our pride and accepting free forgiveness.

The Holy Spirit, the second gift, is the new nature that is offered to us. The Holy Spirit is neither a spirit like one of the dangerous demons feared by worshipers in some primitive religions nor a spirit in the mystical sense of an ineffable divine mist or fragrance—though that reflects a little of the truth. The Holy Spirit is a member of the Trinity, one of the three persons of the Godhead, the Comforter Jesus promised to leave behind Him. At Pentecost, He fell upon the eager crowd. *He* is the correct word, for the Holy Spirit is personal. You see, God is personal, and the Holy Spirit is God.

And so the gift of the Spirit imparts to us

the nature of Jesus Himself. He comes not to stand over us as a challenge or in front of us as an example but to live in us as a vibrant new life.

Is this hard to understand? If so, don't be dismayed; the Trinity is the deepest area of Christian truth, full of mystery. The good news is, you don't have to understand it! Just think of the extraordinary power and conviction that transformed a terrified bunch of disorganized disciples, their leader disgraced and crucified, into a body of bold preachers and fearless missionaries who changed the world. That's the Holy Spirit at work! Just look at the radical change of life that takes place in everyone who truly accepts Jesus Christ as Savior and Lord. That's the Holy Spirit at work as well!

Receive His Spirit

The really breathtaking thing about God's offer to us is this: He is willing to put the same Holy Spirit who empowered Jesus into the hearts and lives of all people who will receive

Him. And that is the essence of becoming a real Christian.

We may be decent, good family people. We may be baptized, confirmed churchgoers. But if we have not received the spirit of Jesus into our lives, the New Testament makes it very plain that we are not yet Christians.

Jesus Himself offers a wonderfully clear picture of what is needed for us to receive His spirit: "Behold, I stand at the door and knock. If anyone hears My voice and opens the door, I will come in to him and dine with him, and he with Me" (Rev. 3:20). It has helped thousands to faith.

To invite the spirit of Jesus to come and share our lives is a *reasonable* thing to do. He has proved His love by dying for us.

It is a *simple* thing to do. Anyone can open a door and let a visitor in.

It is a *necessary* thing to do. He has to be welcomed in before any real relationship can begin.

It is an *urgent* thing to do. If you hear His knock and do nothing, you will not find it so easy to respond to His call the next time. So why not do it now?

Welcome the Holy Spirit into your life. Tell Him you are sorry you have kept Him out so long. Let Him know that from now on you are surrendering your whole life into His hands.

Have you asked Him in? He did not promise that you would immediately feel different or act differently. He *did* promise that He would come in. And if you have asked Him, He *has done* just that. Not because you and I deserve it, but because He promised, and He cannot and will not break His word. That is what faith is, initially. It is taking Him at His word and counting on its reliability!

8
What Next?

If you have entrusted your life to God by welcoming the spirit of Jesus into your heart, you have made the most important of all decisions. What is it going to mean for the days ahead?

A New Relationship

One of the best ways to build any relationship is to spend time together. But how can we do that with God? Prayer and Scripture are two of the main ways.

Prayer is essentially talking to God and listening for His voice. We can call for help, express our gratitude, or simply tell Him that we love Him. Gradually, as we grow in the

Christian life, we will learn to discern His guidance as He seeks to teach and encourage us.

The Scriptures carry God's message for the world. Though written by many individuals, there was only one source of inspiration: God. Read a bit of the Bible every day, and ask God to speak to you personally through its pages. It is a marvelous way to develop your relationship with Him as well as learn a great deal about Him and His ways.

Why not start your Bible reading with one of the four Gospels or one of the short epistles in the New Testament—Philippians, 1 John, or 2 Timothy? Then ask your local minister or a Christian bookstore to help you choose a simple system of regular Bible readings. Bible reading systems such as the lectionary in the Book of Common Prayer, Ligonier Ministries' "Table Talk," Back to the Bible's "Our Daily Bread," or "Read Your Bible Through in a Year" found in many Nelson Bibles might be helpful.

A New Confidence

We are not left in doubt about whether we are in God's family or not. We are intended to know where we stand. And the Holy Spirit not only comes into our lives but assures us that we belong.

He does so in a variety of ways. The New Testament tells of a new joy He imparts, a new love for fellow Christians, an enhanced compassion for those in need, a new experience of receiving answers to our prayers, and a new peace as we go about our daily business. These marks of the new life do not all happen at once. Give them time! But in particular, the Holy Spirit gradually enhances our confidence in two ways.

First, He gives us a new power to overcome temptation if we ask for it. It is the power of Jesus' life in us, no less. And over the years that provides a real transformation of character.

And when we fail, as we often do, the Holy Spirit reminds us of the way back: "If we confess our sins, He is faithful and just to forgive us our sins and to cleanse us from all unrighteousness" (1 John 1:9). What confidence that inspires!

A New Family

When you come to Christ, you immediately find yourself in a great family. Several things are rather significant about this family.

You should demonstrate your belonging to the family by being baptized. It is a decisive mark of membership. If you have been baptized already, you don't need to do it again. But you do need to reaffirm publicly those vows of Christian commitment made for you as an infant or by you, perhaps, when you did not mean them.

You should take your place at the family table. Jesus, in the bread and wine of Communion, has left us a marvelous meal by which to remember Him and to draw upon His strength.

You should meet with the family. Family gatherings are important. In most parts of the world they happen on Sundays in church. You can join with others to worship the heavenly Father, learn His ways, pray together, and be renewed by Him in the bonds of family love. The Bible does not conceive of a solitary Christian separated by choice from the fellowship of other believers and worshipers. You are part of a family. Enjoy it!

A New Task

God has a job for us to do. In part, that job is allowing His spirit to change our lives for the better so that we are a good advertisement for Him in our daily work, family life, and relationships in general.

Another part of our job is to work for God's causes of honesty, justice, peacemaking, and compassion wherever we can. Christians are called to seek justice for the oppressed, maintain integrity in personal and public life, help the poor and the sick, and care for the environment. Throughout the long history of campaigns for social reform, Christians have generally been in the forefront, seeking to put into practice God's agenda of righteousness, justice, and liberty.

God wants His church to be more than a gathering on Sunday. He wants us to be a task force on Monday, carrying the values of His kingdom into our world. He wants us, too, to be His business representatives, unembarrassed to belong to His firm and enthusiastic in inviting others to join it.

The marvelous thing is, if we ask God what particular areas He wants to involve us in, He has His own way of showing us.

A New Destiny

God gives us the first installment of His divine life when we open up our hearts and lives to the Holy Spirit. But divine life does not end there. God will not forsake us when we die. We are precious to Him, and He will not scrap the people He died to win. He will welcome us into His presence forever.

So when disaster strikes, when loved ones die, when we face death ourselves, it is not the end. We do not go out like a light when we die. We step over the threshold into the fuller light of God's presence.

The last book of the Bible gives us a vivid picture of what eternal life with God will be like. It tells us that God has wonderful things in store for His people, that believers will be profoundly and eternally happy with Him, and that the pains and struggles of this life will fade into insignificance:

"Behold, the tabernacle of God is with men, and He will dwell with them, and they shall be His people. God Himself will be with them and be their God. And God will wipe away every tear from their eyes; there shall be no more death, nor sorrow, nor crying. There shall be no more pain, for the former things have passed away."

Then He who sat on the throne said, "Behold, I make all things new. . . . I am the Alpha and the Omega, the Beginning and the End. I will give of the fountain of the water of life freely to him who thirsts. He who overcomes shall inherit all things, and I will be his God and he shall be My son" (Rev. 21:3–7).

That's what awaits you and me if we can say with conviction and sincerity that God is, indeed, our God!

8/2004   1/6   3/4